LIVING ON THE EDGE

Sermons for Pentecost (Middle Third)
Cycle C First Lesson Texts

BY R. KEITH HAMMER

C.S.S Publishing Co., Inc.
Lima, Ohio

LIVING ON THE EDGE

Sermons for Pentecost (Middle Third)
Cycle C First Lesson Texts

BY R. KEITH HAMMER

LIVING ON THE EDGE

Copyright © 1991 by
The C.S.S. Publishing Company, Inc.
Lima, Ohio

All rights reserved. No part of this publication may be reproduced, stored in a retrieval system, or transmitted in any form or by any means, electronic, mechanical, photocopying, recording, or otherwise, without the prior permission of the publisher. Inquiries should be addressed to: The C.S.S. Publishing Company, Inc., 628 South Main Street, Lima, Ohio 45804.

Library of Congress Cataloging-in-Publication Data

Hammer, R. Keith, 1945-
    Living on the edge : sermons for Pentecost (middle third) : cycle C first lesson texts / by R. Keith Hammer.
      p.   cm.
    ISBN 1-55673-320-8
    1. Pentecost season — Sermons.   2. Sermons, American.   I. Title
BV4300.5.H35   1991
252'.6—dc20   91-671
                                                                       CIP

9141 / ISBN 1-55673-320-8   PRINTED IN U.S.A.

To
Kristin, Erik and Bjorn
who daily bring much
joy into my life.

Table Of Contents

Introduction   11

Proper 11   13
Pentecost 9
Ordinary Time 16
    Living By A Hunch
    2 Kings 4:8-17

Proper 12   17
Pentecost 10
Ordinary Time 17
    The Gift That Keeps On Giving
    2 Kings 5:1-15ab

Proper 13   23
Pentecost 11
Ordinary Time 18
    When One Is Better Than Many
    2 Kings 13:14-20a

Proper 14   27
Pentecost 12
Ordinary Time 19
    Who's In Charge Here?
    Jeremiah 18:1-11

Proper 15   31
Pentecost 13
Ordinary Time 20
    "Lucky" Is The Saddest Word
    Jeremiah 20:7-13

Proper 16   35
Pentecost 14
Ordinary Time 21
    The Rose Pales
    Jeremiah 28:1-9

Proper 17 39
Pentecost 15
Ordinary Time 22
    This Life Is Yours To Live!
    Ezekiel 18:1-9, 25-29

Proper 18 45
Pentecost 16
Ordinary Time 23
    Take Care Of Each Other!
    Ezekiel 33:1-11

Proper 19 49
Pentecost 17
Ordinary Time 24
    Find Your Way Home
    Hosea 4:1-3; 5:15—6:6

Proper 20 53
Pentecost 18
Ordinary Time 25
    The Soft-touch God
    Hosea 11:1-11

A Note Concerning Lectionaries And Calendars 58

Bibliography 61

All texts in this book are from the series for Lesson One, Common Lectionary. Lutheran and Roman Catholic designations indicate days comparable to Sundays on which Common Lectionary Propers are used.

Introduction

It is here in these latter days of the 20th century that it often feels like we are living on the edge of something. Some days seem like it is the edge of despair where our own self indulgences and the enormity of the problems of the world around us have finally overcome us and we are ready to drop off. On other days it seems like the edge of a new world where a new understanding and co-operative spirit among the peoples of the world together with the advancing gifts of modern technology will bring us new wings and we are ready to lift upward.

Whichever way you see it, I suspect you will agree that living on the edge calls for fresh words of judgment and hope for those of us who are called to preach the good news of our Lord Jesus Christ.

The texts for this middle third of the Pentecost season, Cycle C, from the Common Lectionary afford us the opportunity to engage again the timeless messages of judgment and hope delivered to us by several of the major prophetic voices in the Old Testament. A majority of these texts leave us no doubt that God was not pleased with much of what he saw happening in the lives of his chosen people at that time. My hunch is that, if we can stand the truth, God is not pleased with much of what he sees going on in our lives and time either.

These texts offer us a singular opportunity both to identify the sins of this generation and also to see with eyes of wonder the unending love of our God who keeps pleading for us to come back to him and the life he has for us regardless of what edge we live on. Whatever edge it is, God was there first.

R. Keith Hammer
Pentecost 1990

Proper 11
Pentecost 9
Ordinary Time 16
2 Kings 4:8-17

Living By A Hunch

She was the most respected girls' basketball coach Hankins High had ever had. Not only had her teams compiled the best record in the whole state during her 12-year tenure, but she was popular with all of her students as a teacher as well. She was one of those relatively rare persons who could bring out the best in almost every person she taught or coached.

What made her do it, few people understood. It was in the midst of the pressures of the basketball season where her team was again headed for the state playoffs. But two of her key players were just barely eligible to play. So she passed them in her class when they really had failed. A jealous player who hadn't made the team found out and reported it to the superintendent who immediately suspended her and later fired her.

He was a stranger in town. He came seeking any kind of work and found a job as a common laborer for the city. He worked hard, took part in all the community activities, and gave unselfishly of his time and money to community projects. Soon he was a foreman, then he got an office job for the city. A local businessman liked what he was doing so well he lured him away from his city job to work as his general manager. Soon he was elected to city council and from there he became the mayor. Then a reporter for the local newspaper put a magnifying glass to his past. He discovered the stranger who eventually became the mayor had a long criminal record before coming to the town and had spent 12 years in prison.

How do you make up your mind about people? How do you decide whether a person is trustworthy? Have you ever known a person like the coach who had great respect and then greatly disappointed you? Or have you ever known a person like the laborer who worked his way up to become mayor despite his criminal past?

We live in a time when these kinds of dilemmas are everyday occurrences. How many times a month do you read in the paper of someone who was trusted who took advantage of the trust? Or someone who rose to prominence and turned out to be an impostor?

In our text for today, the rich woman from Shunem confronts just such a dilemma when she befriends Elisha the prophet. Our text gives us the impression that he was a mystery person to her. Yes, they quickly became good friends, but apparently Elisha didn't talk much about what he did when he wasn't in Shunem and apparently the woman didn't ask him for an answer.

But Elisha kept coming back to visit her and her husband. It appears that Elisha was always welcomed. So he began to become a part of her life and she was forced to form some kind of opinion of him.

Just how she did it we do not know. Perhaps it was in Elisha's demeanor that he was so confident a person, so compelling in the way he stated his beliefs about God, that this woman could not help but believe he was a holy man.

Imagine if my glasses this morning were rose-colored. If they were, it would be a message that all of us look at the world and every other person who lives in it from our own unique perspective.

This woman becomes an example of faith for us because she used the gifts of perception God had given her to see Elisha for whom he really was. She perceived he was a man sent from God and she and her husband honored him by building a special room for him and his servant Gehazi to stay each time they were in town. Through Elisha, God returned the favor and gave her and her husband the son for which they had longed all their lives.

We learn from this lady of Shunem just how important it is that we let God give us eyes of faith too as we see the world and all the people who live in it with us.

In Jesus' day, when people saw persons who had leprosy, many turned and ran the other way. In our day, when some persons come to know of someone who has AIDS, that person is often shunned. And yet we today realize how misplaced their fear was. I have a hunch that the same is true for many of us today regarding AIDS. To be sure, it is a dreadful disease, but persons who have it do not deserve the shunning they often get.

The same, to a lesser extent, could be said of people who are homeless or people who have certain kinds of physical handicaps. When helping them to have a better life seems so overwhelming to us, it is easy for us to throw up our hands and walk the other way.

Yes, rose-colored glasses, symbolic of the way we see the world and most especially our human sisters and brothers who live in it, can lead us to pretend not to see many who would very much like our love and compassion.

Today we have the example of a great lady who was different. She perceived the inner being of Elisha the man of God and honored him. That was truly a wonderful gift of faith which God gave her.

You and I are given the same kind of gift as we have been baptized. It is the gift of seeing beyond the outward appearances of our human sisters and brothers to the persons inside who want as much to be affirmed, valued, and respected as any one of us does.

Sometimes, through many experiences when their self-worth has been put down, many people do not reveal this inner desire to anyone. Rather, they will strike out and hurt others.

It takes someone with a mature gift of faith to see the child of God inside such persons.

That, I believe, is just what God calls us to do. Take away the blinders, or the rose-colored glasses, that allow us to see only what we choose to see. Then turn to our Lord and ask him to let you see his child in every person you meet.

Then you will know what the love of God is like. For to receive this way of looking at other people, you will have to open yourself to be seen in just that way by them.

May God open all of our eyes to see the "loved and lovable" person inside each person we meet every day! Amen.

Proper 12
Pentecost 10
Ordinary Time 17
2 Kings 5:1-15ab

The Gift That Keeps On Giving

It is a hectic Sunday morning after worship. People are streaming in and out of the pastor's office as he tries to put away all of the things that seem to have accumulated on his desk since he arrived earlier that morning. Suddenly Neta appears at the door. "Pastor, I'd like you to meet Emily Johnson. She's worshiping with us for the first time today and wants to join our church."

The pastor puts aside what he is doing and greets Emily warmly. He invites her to sit down for a minute so that he can get to know her a little better. Emily begins to tell the pastor how much she likes the congregation. She was especially impressed with the Sunday school for her three young children. She wants to join soon so that they can get started regularly and wonders what she needs to do to join. She isn't a member of this church's denomination and hasn't attended church regularly since she was a teenager.

She reaches in a bag that she has with her and brings out a watercolor painting which she has painted herself. "Here," she says, "I have a gift I want to give you since you're going to be my pastor."

The pastor is a bit surprised, but he receives the gift graciously. Already he is getting restless. It has been a long morning and he would like to get home for lunch and relax a little before the denominational meeting he has to attend that afternoon.

Then Emily tells him that she is a single parent and has just started back to school to finish her degree which will take her about two years. She is on a limited budget and she has heard that the church is a place to go to find people who are willing to help when you need help. She wonders if the pastor could help her find someone who would babysit for her for free.

Now, if you were the pastor, how would you respond to Emily?

Perhaps Emily's story is not so different from Naaman's story in our text for today. We all know Naaman's story from our Sunday school days. It is one of the more familiar stories in the Old Testament.

Naaman is a foreigner to the king of Israel, yes, even a sometime enemy. But here he comes bearing gifts, seeking a favor from the king. He wants the king to heal him of his leprosy.

The king of Israel at the time shows us one way to respond to Emily. We could respond with offense. "What do you think this place is? A welfare agency? Lady, have you gotten the wrong information about what is going on here."

The king doesn't understand at all what Naaman's request is. He knows that he has no special power to heal anyone of leprosy. He becomes very suspicious, suggesting that really what Naaman wants him to do is reject him, so that he (Naaman) can become offended and have reason to start a quarrel with him.

This part of this story lifts up for us a dilemma which constantly faces us in the church. How do we respond to those who come to us seeking some kind of help for themselves or members of their family — sometimes even bearing us gifts and flattering us in the process?

This is every church's challenge.

One of the groups of persons I think of immediately here are the transients who come to the church seeking help. Most often they come directly to me and ask for a handout. Usually they describe a very urgent need which they have for food, rent money, or perhaps gas to get to another town. Sometimes they even promise to send me the money when they get their welfare check. How am I to judge whether these people are telling the truth or not? If you were in my shoes, how would you respond?

Another group of people are people like Emily. They come with a need but they are looking for more than just the immediate filling of their need. They do want a place to belong, a place that will give them support, but sometimes, like Emily, the need or needs they have are great.

Still another group of people are those who come and want to get involved in the church right away. It's easy for us to become excited about them because we are always looking for volunteers and when people offer without having to be asked, it is a special pleasure. Yet, often many of these people overextend themselves or have various kinds of problems relating to the persons with whom they work so that their helping becomes more of a burden than a sharing in the work of the church.

These are the people God sends us to whom we are called to minister. I am not sure that we often see them as such. Very often, I suspect, we see many of these persons more as "problem" prospective members rather than persons to welcome into the family with open arms.

In our text the prophet Elisha was the person who offered the real welcome for Naaman and offered to fill the request which he brought. Notice that Elisha didn't make much to-do about all the gifts Naaman brought him. It appears that he saw Naaman himself as the real gift God had sent him. Here was a man, who once he was healed, would become a witness for God's power among a group of foreigners — even sometime enemies.

Naaman at first didn't like the way the offer of healing was extended to him. Many of the persons who come to us with needs often at first don't like the way we extend our friendship to them either. But in the end he received the gift of healing, and he exclaims with joy, "Now I know there is no god but the God of Israel."

Today this text affords our congregation the opportunity to reflect on how we receive persons who come to us seeking our help. Sometimes, they, like Naaman, come bearing material gifts, hoping as I'm sure Naaman hoped, that nice gifts will get our attention and lead us to fill their perceived needs.

How easy it is for us to reject both their gift and them. Often it is not apparent to us how we can meet their immediate needs. Certainly we don't want to give the impression either that we can be bribed or, for that matter, that it is necessary to bring a gift to get our help.

How easy it is for us, like the king, to miss the real dynamic of what is happening when these persons come to us. Really, you see, as Elisha rightly perceived the persons themselves are the real gifts from God. If we can find a way to receive them (and often that means addressing their immediate needs) not only will we have responded with God's love and mercy, but more than likely we will have received a gift that keeps on giving.

Imagine how many people Naaman told about what happened to him, giving praise to God when he arrived home. Truly he was a gift to Israel who kept on giving for many years into the future.

That's who the persons are who come to us bearing gifts and needs. They are God's gifts to us through whom we can fulfill his call to show love, mercy and forgiveness to all.

Here's what the pastor did for Emily. He told her that he would think about her need and how the church could help her and call her back at a time they agreed. That evening he called Mabel Black whose only daughter and family had moved half a continent away. Mabel had been so involved with her grandchildren that she was having a really difficult time adjusting. Mabel was on Emily's doorstep the next morning. Not only did Emily join the congregation and become an active, ministering member herself, but she brought her brother and his family, her sister and her family, and a close friend and her family into membership in the church, too. She became a gift that kept on giving even as she received a gift that kept on giving.

We can be that kind of a congregation, too. I hope that seeing Naaman's story from another perspective this morning will help you as members of our congregation to give more careful thought to the persons who come to us with needs. Almost every time we can find a way to meet them through prayer, patience, and creative problem-solving. Then we too will have among us many new gifts who keep on giving. Amen.

Proper 13
Pentecost 11
Ordinary Time 18
2 Kings 13:14-20a

When One Is Better Than Many

Recently I heard a radio commercial by a well-known travel service. In the ad a neighbor asks the man in the family if he is moving when he sees him get in a large flatbed truck with a tow truck on the back. No, the man replies, they are just going on a vacation and his wife is afraid of breakdowns so they are bringing their own tow truck along. Then the neighbor asks whom the uniformed man is standing near the truck. The man says that he is Bill, the security guard, who they are taking along to guard their money. Then the neighbor starts to tell them about the travel service and how both of these needs will be met just by joining it. They will have a toll-free number to call for help if they have a breakdown, free travelers' checks and they can even get free maps. With that the man gets all excited and yells to his wife that she can let the bloodhounds go.

Of course, this is a humorous exaggeration of the services provided by this travel service, but I thought of it when I read the way that Jehoash reacted to Elisha's impending death in our text for today.

Jehoash is terribly upset when he learns that Elisha is dying. But he is not upset because he is losing a good friend. He is upset because he realizes that soon he will not have his best protection against his enemies.

The humorous part of it is that he has all the protection he needs. He has many horse-drawn chariots and great armies with powerful bows and arrows to defend him. If there was ever a king who could be confident in the power of his armies, it should have been Jehoash.

But to the contrary, he is, as some might say, a "basket case."

What was going on with Jehoash?

Of course, we don't know all the details. But from the way Elisha handles this situation, we can speculate with a high degree of confidence as to what it was.

Jehoash was a king who had to have the best of everything. He needed many horse-drawn chariots, so he got them. He needed huge armies armed with the latest and most powerful bows and arrows. What the king wanted, he made sure that he had. But most of all, Jehoash, in his friendship with Elisha, realized he had the "secret weapon" — Elisha's advice and mysterious, but unequaled power. Following Elisha's guidance, he couldn't lose.

But what was he to do when he lost the cornerstone of his defense? Well, here he is — the great king — weeping uncontrollably.

I suspect that many of us could see ourselves in Jehoash's shoes. What do you do when you face the threat of losing that which you hold dearest?

For many of us that would be the loss of a family member or close friend. Our loss would be a genuine one — losing a person we love and who may have been a partner or helpmate for us.

But to go beyond that, the question is: How much of your way of living could you lose without falling apart?

So often our lives are guided by the principle that more is better. If it's cheaper to buy 25 pounds of potatoes than five pounds, we buy the 25 if we have the room. If it's convenient to have two cars in the family or even one for each driver if there are more than two drivers, we find a way to purchase them. Even in our spiritual lives today, we can avail ourselves of a half-dozen versions of the Bible to be able to understand it better.

After a while, you see, we become dependent upon having more than one choice or more than one option for almost every aspect of our lives.

You have all received slick fliers which come in almost every bill you receive these days. Temptations are all around us to purchase more and more — perhaps even more than we can afford to buy.

Our society today encourages us in such a lifestyle. We have many things from which to choose, whether we are outfitting our wardrobe, purchasing a new car, or even choosing a church to attend. And in many cases, the message is clear: If you can't decide, take them all.

Elisha had a last and, he hoped, lasting gift to leave with Jehoash. He wanted him to see his way out of his dire dilemma.

You recall our text. He had Jehoash go and get his bow and some arrows. He had Jehoash take out one arrow. Elisha carefully helped the king line up his arrow and get it as close to perfect in his bow as he could. Then he opened the window and told the king to shoot the arrow. The arrow went straight to its target.

Elisha said something to this effect, "See what just happened. You took your time to line up the arrow and aim it. It went straight to its mark. So it is with you. You are the Lord's arrow. When you take time to listen to what God expects of you, you will accomplish his purposes and there is nothing that shall stop you. You will have victory over Syria and all your enemies. Now take the rest of your arrows out and destroy them."

The king went out and destroyed some, but he just could not bring himself to destroy all of them. He needed to hold back some for his own security.

There is a clear and potent message for all of us who live by faith in our Lord Jesus Christ. When God calls us to faith, he calls us to turn from the many competing voices of our lives, each of which say they have the answer or part of it and to give our lives to him as the only source of guidance and power for living. When God is God for us, he takes over and assures us that he will be with us so that we will overcome all the adversities that face us and enjoy the forgiveness, love, joy, and peace that he alone can give! That's it! With God one is better than many.

Sadly, Jehoash couldn't learn soon enough and so his life and power were diminished.

It is not too late for you and me. If we don't need the items in these slick fliers, we can say "no" and throw them in the wastebasket. God calls us to take a look at our lives and see how we can learn to choose only what we need for a good life under his guidance. This is a way of focusing on what our real values are and giving more time to letting them enhance and enliven our days. When we trust in God above everything else, less is definitely better. Making good use of the fewer things we have which we really value leads to spiritual fulfillment and wholeness.

Choose who you will serve. Let it be God and him alone! Amen.

Proper 14
Pentecost 12
Ordinary Time 19
Jeremiah 18:1-11

Who's In Charge Here?

Anyone who works in a hospital emergency room can relate many stories of persons who come in under emergency situations and have suffered what appears to be a heart attack or have stopped breathing for other reasons. They are put on a breathing machine.

Some of these persons do not regain consciousness even after they are put on the breathing machine. Then after a period of days or sometimes weeks the doctor and family must make the decision to remove the machine. Often it means that the person will not breathe on his or her own and thus die.

Reaching the decision to remove the machine is always a very difficult and painful decision for the family members to make. It often seems to them, emotionally at least, as if they are causing the end of the life of their loved one.

Of course, this is not true. In our text for today we have a clear declaration by the prophet Jeremiah that our lives are finally in God's hands and he is the one who decides when we will be born and is there to preside when our lives end, too.

However, the advances of modern technological medicine have raised some very serious and deep questions about how much doctors and family members should have to say about ending the life of a person who cannot let their own wishes be known.

Who should have the final say? Who is the one who should finally determine when the switch is turned off the breathing machine or the plug is pulled to stop it? The doctor? The family? Or perhaps even the government?

The setting of our text for today has little relationship to the setting of a modern medical facility, but the root issue which Jeremiah, speaking for God, was confronting in the people was not all that different.

Here we once again have the picture of God's wayward people. Oh, they certainly didn't think they were wayward people. They actually believed that their superior knowledge and experience led them to make decisions and take actions which were superior to anything God could do. After all, they lived on the earth, they tilled it, they cared for the animals who provided meat and clothing, they established towns and cities. And God — where was he? They never saw him. So it was natural for them to want to do things their own way.

You have to admit that it was a pretty arrogant attitude that these people had. And they continued to show how stubborn they could be. In no way would they turn and acknowledge their sinfulness.

The parallel I see between the people of Israel and those in a modern hospital who have to make a life and death decision is that it is easy to slip into the belief that they alone are actually making these decisions.

The decision they have made is to use a machine that for many people has great therapeutic value. There are dozens of persons in any hospital who thank God that there was a breathing machine to help them breathe or even breathe for them when they needed it. But to suppose that this machine or any others of the "miracle" machines of modern medicine give us the power to have control over life and death is just not true.

Jeremiah reminded the wayward people of his day that just as they had come from the dust of the earth, they were still like clay in the hands of a potter to God. When the potter doesn't like what he is making, he flattens the clay and starts over. God could surely do that too when he discovered that his children were wandering too far from the way of life he intended them to lead.

This could seem like a very harsh word. But certainly it need not be received as such. Through Jeremiah, God also reminds the people that he is even more willing to forgive them and help them shape their lives into the kind of lives he had envisioned his people to have. He urges Jeremiah to call them to repentance so that he (God) can shape them with his creative spirit into the persons he intended them to be in the first place.

Certainly we need to be reminded of whom our God is as we struggle with the many dilemmas with which modern technological medicine has confronted us.

Yes, we are responsible to be the very best caretakers we can be of the lives and gifts God has given us. But God is still very clearly in charge of our comings and our goings.

At those times when the momentous decision to remove life support systems is being made, there is often a chorus of persons, including doctors and nurses, who join in reassuring families that they are not making the decision as to whether their loved one dies or lives. Each person is still very clearly in the hands of God, who accompanies her from her very last breath into eternity.

But there is mercy and abundant goodness when our lives are in God's hands too. Most of the time, death, when it comes after a breathing machine has been removed, is quiet and peaceful.

Let us affirm today that even though we now have machines, which can prolong our lives past the time we normally would die and have the power to turn these machines on and off, still our lives finally are in God's hands.

Still he is the potter, and we are the clay. Still God is in charge of our world and all of us in it. Still we live by the gift of faith so as to learn more fully the spiritual dimensions of this life we have been given.

Let this sermon be the occasion for you to think about and discuss with your loved ones how you feel about the use of life support systems. But as you do, do so with much prayer and a healthy dose of awe that it is really God who gives us life and every good and meaningful experience in it! Amen.

Proper 15
Pentecost 13
Ordinary Time 20
Jeremiah 20:7-13

"Lucky" Is The Saddest Word

I race off to the convenience mart a few blocks from my home to pick up some milk for cereal for breakfast. I hurriedly go to the dairy case and snatch two plastic gallon jugs and turn for the checkout to pay for them.

Suddenly I am confronted by "The Machine." "The Machine" in this case isn't a machine at all. It's a huge display which overpowers everything else near the checkout, telling me that I can get all of the tickets for all of the state lottery games now at this store. All I have to do is hand over a buck or two of the change I will have anyway from the $10 bill I give the checkout lady and I am in business.

"The Machine," if there is one, and its accompanying displays always tell me how much I can win. A cool $6 million if I am lucky in the "Super Lotto" drawing. But there are hundreds of other prizes, from thousands of dollars to just another ticket of some kind to keep my habit going.

I have a hunch that preaching against the lottery and other games of chance like it is not a very popular subject today. All of us participate sometimes, even if we don't play the lottery. We take part when we purchase tickets for raffles held by various community groups, sometimes even churches.

I picked the subject because I believe that in a certain sense preaching against lotteries, raffles and games of chance is much like the message delivered by Jeremiah the prophet in our text for today.

Jeremiah delivered a message of judgment upon the people of Israel who had taken to worshiping other gods. They were so caught up in their way of life centering around this worship that they thought everything was going just fine and that God, if he really cared, must be quite satisfied with them. Nothing could have been much further from the truth.

So it was that Jeremiah brought a scathing word of judgment. It was meant to be so harsh that it might just shock the people into really taking a look at what they were doing.

But it didn't seem to work that way for most of the people. Rather than frightening the people, it brought them to great anger and they had Jeremiah locked up in the stocks where they could ridicule him all the day long.

It seemed so inappropriate to stir up all this trouble when life was moving along merrily and people were having so much fun.

Could the same be said to be true today concerning the lottery, raffles and other games of chance in which we partake? After all, many of them are so innocent and often they raise money for a good cause.

What we must understand is that there was a deeper reason for Jeremiah's heavy protestations than just trying to spoil the people's fun. Jeremiah spoke a word that the Lord had laid upon his heart. He says that it was a message like a "fire burning deep within me." He could see how their apostasy was leading them toward a situation where their good life would be destroyed and they would be led away into exile.

I believe it's time that we who claim Jesus as our Lord and Savior take another look at our participation in all kinds of games of chance. It has become a much deeper issue than one of simple morality — that is, that it's sinful to gamble.

What is happening to our society is that we are stampeding toward a society where wealth and comfortable lifestyles rule for many at the expense of a larger segment of our people who underwrite the easy living for the rest of society.

Consider how lotteries, raffles and games of chance play into this style of life. There is the underlying idea that you can be "lucky" and gain a great prize which will give you much material wealth. But who is it that pays the price for the few lucky ones who win the top prize? Of course, all of the rest of us who purchase the other tickets.

The argument can be made that we purchase the tickets willingly. So we do, but often with the aid of our weaker nature which would rather take the easy way to a comfortable life rather than putting forth the effort to give some of ourselves for what we receive.

If the current trends continue, we are rushing toward more contests with huge prizes. The greater the prize, the more the players — so the common wisdom goes. But with more big winners, we also have thousands, even millions of losers.

From a particular Christian perspective, all of this lust for being lucky discourages the Christian idea of stewardship. We are called to care for what God has given us, use what we need, but also to share with others so that we all may have a good life.

Just as Jeremiah spoke the word of the Lord to the unfaithful ones in his day, we need to hear it today from the heart of God's love.

God says to you and me, "You don't have to be lucky to live. Your being here is not a matter of chance. I chose and fashioned you in your mother's womb and I have a purpose for you far beyond being "lucky" or based on the value of your net worth. The life I have for you is a life to be shared in a community where people forgive, care for, and love one another. It has much deeper rewards than winning any prize will ever have."

It's time to ask: Where are you on this matter? Are you one who is sitting back now chuckling to yourself because the pastor got all worked up because people are having a little fun with legal games of chance? Or do you join me in my concern that the mass marketing of this way of life of the "lucky" is seriously masking the good news of our Lord Jesus?

I am convinced that we who follow Jesus need to lift up the whole sense of the care of creation and our own personal resources which we have come to know in the biblical way of faith. It is time to show that this stewardship begins with the giving of ourselves and the gifts we have been given and showing this as we reach out to help others and share what God has given us.

This message is from the heart of God. It is similar to the one Jeremiah tried to proclaim in his day. I hope that more people are willing to receive it and let it change their lives today than did in the time of Jeremiah. But even if few will receive it, still it is a word I feel compelled to proclaim as God's Word burns within me. I hope you will find it to be so for you, too. Amen.

Proper 16
Pentecost 14
Ordinary Time 21
Jeremiah 28:1-9

The Rose Pales

Who is fit to speak for God? This is not an academic or philosophical question. It is the question which the church must ask again and again as it chooses its pastors and leaders.

In our denomination a person who wants to be a pastor has to go through a lengthy process to become recognized and ordained by the church. *(Modify this paragraph to fit your denomination's practices.)* That lengthy process includes meeting with several committees for extended periods of time over several years. It also includes taking a specialized course of study at a seminary to learn in depth the Bible, our theology, our heritage, pastoral care, and many other practical aspects of leadership in the church. A person who successfully completes this long process is recognized as a person who can speak for God from our pulpits.

Who is fit to speak for God? Our pastors, you say. But how can you be sure? Or for that matter how can the church itself be sure? Does even this long process of learning and maturation in Christian faith qualify a person to speak for God?

In our lesson today we have a struggle between two prophets who both claimed they spoke for God. One was a preacher who seemed to be preaching "hell and damnation." He told the people that they were going to be led into exile because they refused to listen to God's warnings and repent and meanwhile continued on their own jolly good way of sinful living. The other preacher proclaimed his message emphasizing the positive events he believed would soon take place. He said he knew things had been rough when the Babylonians had marched in and cleaned out the temple "lock, stock and barrel," but he assured the people that if they had a little patience and began to think positively, within two years their travail would be over.

Now, to which of these two preachers would you like to listen? Which one do you think would give you more hope and reason to go on living in a very difficult time? Which one of these preachers, therefore, must be the one who speaks for God?

If your answer is the second one, you are wrong, as you probably have already guessed. This one was Hananiah. He was the people's choice because he seemed to bring them some hope.

The one who spoke for God was the first one — Jeremiah. The words of his prophecy make up one of the books of the Old Testament.

Now let me ask you again: Who is fit to speak for God? If the majority of us had picked Hananiah and are wrong, how can we be so sure that we can really judge the qualifications of any person to speak for God?

There is an answer for us. It is right here in the text. But it is not an obvious answer, one in fact that many of us as church leaders, pastors, and lay persons in the church today may miss.

Perhaps it can best be explained by considering the story of Hank.

Hank as a young man was full of much enthusiasm for God. He decided he wanted to be a pastor. He went to seminary and graduated with many commendations for his work and personality for ministry. He went to his first parish and did not disappoint those who had great expectations for him. If there was ever a pastor who could have been said to have begun his ministry with the color and passion of a deep red rose, it was Hank.

In a few years after having led the congregation to much growth in size and faith, he moved on to another congregation. This was a large one with greater challenges, but those did not stop Hank. He continued to grow as an outstanding young pastor in his church. Soon there was a third parish, a large one with a staff ministry and Hank came as associate, but moved up to be the senior pastor when the pastor he was working with retired.

Something started to happen to Hank. Nobody noticed it much at first, but he just wasn't quite as prompt at getting things done and keeping appointments as he once had been. He started spending more time on the golf course and at the race track than he did preparing his sermons or visiting the hospitalized. Gradually it got worse. His closest friends spoke to Hank about it out of concern for him. His bishop did likewise. But Hank went on his merry way. Soon there was a committee from the bishop's office investigating him. Hank was given the opportunity to make changes or resign. He chose to resign. The community determined that the way Hank had conducted himself in the whole affair was so unbecoming of one who was ordained, so he was stripped of his ordination.

The next five years of Hank's life were ones of continuing descent into the depths of life. He lost his marriage, his family, and most of his earthly possessions. He refused all help. He became a very lonely man.

One day on a visit to his doctor, his doctor came in to Hank's room visibly upset. "I have very bad news," he said. He proceeded to tell Hank that he had a rare, degenerative muscle disease which would probably take his life in five to 10 years, and even the time he had left would be a time of great pain and probable disability.

It was as if Hank had been jolted back to reality. He decided to make amends to all of the people he had wronged. He continued this course with the kind of enthusiasm with which he had begun his ministry. And he went and asked for his ordination back, but the church wouldn't give it to him.

Hank started to write about his life and experiences and his developing terminal illness. He decided to see if his experiences could help others who were facing what he was facing. So he started to counsel persons who faced death or great losses. He formed support groups. He started making speeches telling of his experience. Against the wishes of the bishop, some of the churches he had served invited him back to preach. His messages were so stirring that other churches began to hear of him and invited him to speak, too.

Soon Hank was reaching more people than he had ever reached in his previous ministries. He spoke with great conviction of how he had discovered God's peace and power through the pain and degeneration which was happening in his body. People were so moved because they had no doubts in seeing and hearing Hank that he spoke about what he knew was true. Hank still had some of his outward vigor and handsome qualities. He had become a pale rose, but he still spoke with passion for the God he knew and loved.

Who is fit to speak for God? We in the church will never have an easy answer for this question if we seek to answer it honestly by faith.

Listen carefully to all you hear in the church. Not everyone you hear in this place speaks with the same passion from the heart of God. Not every message which is from the heart of God may be a message you want to hear. Jeremiah and Hank remind us of the truth of both of these statements.

The rose paled in Hank's life, but it was still a rose. Not red, but still a proper symbol of the love and commitment which is ours from the heart of God.

Think of Hank when you see a fading rose. Then know that God's power can come to you even through messengers whose messages have previously been rejected.

You are never too pale for God to listen to you one more time. Amen.

Proper 17
Pentecost 15
Ordinary Time 22
Ezekiel 18:1-9, 25-29

This Life Is Yours To Live!

There is a wonderful device that all of us have in our homes that reveals to us the solution to all of the problems we have in life. Some of you may think I am talking about the Bible, but I am not. While the Bible does reveal to us the spiritual truths that will make our lives whole, there is another more fundamental device that shows us who it is who can solve all of the problems we face every day.

The answer is simple. It is a mirror. If you gaze into it, you will have the answer to all of the problems you will ever face in life. You may think it strange to suggest to you that what you see in a mirror is the answer to all of the problems you will ever face. Yet, what I am doing, I believe, is illustrating the fundamental truth which God is trying to communicate through the prophet Ezekiel in our text this morning.

The people of Israel to whom this text originally was addressed found themselves to be detainees, "guests" who couldn't go home, exiles in a strange land. The armies of Babylonia had swept over their country and led them away into captivity.

Now they were beginning to wonder who was responsible for their being where they were. They couldn't see that they themselves had much to do with it because it had happened so quickly. They really didn't have time to prepare for what was happening or even defend themselves adequately.

Then it dawned on them. The prophets had warned their parents that this would happen, but their parents had not taken heed of what the prophets had said. They found a way of saying that which their captors didn't really understand, but which they themselves understood very well. "The parents (our parents) ate the sour grapes," they said, "But the children (that's us) got the sour taste (it's sour too — we hate this place)." Woe is us. There isn't anything we can do about it now.

And a sorry lot they were. As long as they sat around and felt sorry for themselves and blamed it all on their parents, their situation became even more helpless. They was no one who could help them because the people who were responsible for their being in this strange land were all dead.

If they would only have had a mirror, maybe they would have seen what a great mistake they were making.

But they had something just about as good — maybe even better. They had Ezekiel the prophet who could deliver God's message. Their parents may have all been dead, but God was still sending his prophets to deliver his message.

Ezekiel speaks the word of the Lord and minces no words in delivering his message.

He tells them to stop blaming their parents for their woes. To be sure their parents had not listened at all to what God said to them: they deserved what their children got. But their children were not innocent babes.

For one thing, in their woeful crying in Babylon, they had forgotten who they were. They were God's children and he had promised never to forsake them, even when they were led off to exile. It was also true that they were not as innocent in this matter as they thought they were. Like their parents they had not listened to God very well either. They had had their opportunities to repent and save their land, but they found it easier to follow in the footsteps of their parents. And if they were ever going to get back to their homeland, they would have to take full responsibility for all of the sins that led God to allow them to be led into exile.

Now we begin to see why a mirror is not merely a device of conceit. You and I ourselves are the answer to all the problems we face in life. By the way we manage our lives, we hold the answer to enough of the problems we face everyday to make the difference between a meaningful life and a life which might drive us to suicide. The reason you see is all summed up in this one verse spoken by the prophet for God, "The life of every person belongs to me (that is, God)."

Someone has said that each of us is either a part of the problem or a part of the solution to everything we face in life. That is a very biblical statement according to the words which Ezekiel speaks for God here.

We can choose, like the captives in Babylon, to blame all of our problems on someone else and then we are part of those problems. Or, we can take responsibility for our lives, confess our sins, and seek to fulfill the purpose for which God created each one of us and then we become part of the solution.

When Ezekiel started speaking straight for God, he angered the people and they started to blame God. "What the Sovereign Lord does isn't right," they said. Now they shifted the blame from their parents to God himself.

But it was all for naught. They were doing so to use the common ploy of diversion so that the real source of their problems — themselves and their sins — would not be so apparent.

God pleads with them through Ezekiel, "Turn away from all the evil you are doing, and don't let your sins destroy you. Give up all the evil you have been doing, and get yourselves new minds and hearts . . . I don't want anyone to die." God's promise to them is that once they turn toward him again he will forgive them and so not judge them on their past sins but on their new life of being faithful to God.

God pleads with them to turn from being part of the problems they face and become a part of the solutions. When they realize that they are God's children and that he really does want good for them, then they will realize they need to confess their sins and seek the help only God can give them so that they can begin to solve the problems that surround them.

One of the famous last words which you and I hear repeated time and time again is, "I'm glad that's not my problem." But it is! Every problem is. That does not automatically mean that we interfere in other people's private lives and try to become their savior. But it does mean that because we belong to God, we are called to care and show mercy. Then the phrase, "That's not my problem," will disappear from our lives.

Think for a moment. Is there any problem in the world which could not become your problem? AIDS, homelessness, drugs, cancer — these are some of the most feared situations of life today. While we may not personally be involved in any of them right now, we may know of persons we love and cherish who are. And who knows what tomorrow will bring? It could happen to us even as we think, "No, never, not me!"

It's that way too with all of the smaller problems we face in life. When you are having a difficult time in a relationship, it will go much better if you accept responsibility for your part of the relationship, admit your mistakes and do what you can to make it better. If things are not going well for you at work, if you change the things you can so that you do the best job you can do, more than likely you will make a difference enough so that your job will be better. Here at church if you are not satisfied with what is happening in our ministry, you can do your part to make things better by taking an active part in our ministry and making sure you say only things which will go to strengthen our life together as a congregation. When you become part of the solution, God becomes much more visible in your life.

Today God invites each of us to daily take stock of our lives, confess our sins, not only to him, but those we have hurt by our sins as well, and then seek to find the ways we can become a part of the solutions to as many of the human problems which we encounter directly or indirectly as we can.

Once again we are reminded that living as a Christian may not be the easiest life in the world, but when you think of what the alternatives are, you and I who know and love Jesus as our Lord know it is the best life.

When you look in a mirror, you see there the person who holds the solutions to the problems you and those you touch face in life — you, not as God, not as one lone superperson, but as God's child whom with his Spirit in you can love, forgive, care, show mercy and share joy!

May God empower you to be a part of the solutions to the problems of your life and those with whom you live each day. Amen.

Proper 18
Pentecost 16
Ordinary Time 23
Ezekiel 33:1-11

Take Care Of Each Other!

Once upon a time there were two little boys. They were both basically good little boys, but as boys like to do, they would run far and wide finding "interesting" places to play. Little Jimmy liked to play in the woods. Little Bobby liked to play in the fields, especially where there was lots of dirt.

Jimmy would always bring interesting things from the woods home to show his parents. One time he brought an injured chipmunk which he nursed back to health. At other times he would bring home bouquets of beautiful woodland flowers for his mother. In the fall of the year, he gathered a beautiful collection of colored leaves. Bobby also brought home gifts for his parents. One time he brought home a mud pie which he had made. Another time he brought home a crude car he had fashioned from the clay. He found all kinds of snakes, bugs and worms and he was always bringing some of them home to show his parents. As time went on, it seemed like the parents always liked Jimmy's gifts better than Bobby's gifts. This was really upsetting to Bobby and he began to brood about it. He would even say sometimes to his parents, "How come it is you always like Jimmy's presents and you just throw mine out? Yesterday you put Jimmy's flower on the dinner table and you threw my mud pie in the trash." And his parents assured him that his mud pie was every bit as special as Jimmy's flower. But it sure didn't seem that way to Bobby.

One day Jimmy came to see Bobby in the field where he was playing. They got into a terrible fist fight. Bobby was a little bigger than Jimmy and he began to hit Jimmy pretty hard. Jimmy started to cry but Bobby just kept hitting him.

Suddenly Jimmy fell to the ground, striking his head against a large, sharp rock. Jimmy was very quiet. Bobby ran crying to his parents. They called an ambulance, but it was too late. Jimmy had died.

The parents asked Bobby, "What happened? Why did you fight with Jimmy? Why did you hit him so hard?"

Amidst his tears, Bobby in great fear said, "Why do you ask so many questions? Jimmy could always take care of himself before. He brought you many things which you liked very much. When did you ever tell me I was supposed to be his babysitter?"

I expect that many of you will recognize the story I have just told you as an updated version of a story you learned in Sunday school. It is the story of Cain and Abel and as such it is one of the oldest stories in the Bible. From the very beginning, we who share the Judeo-Christian faith have learned that we are responsible for one another.

This is a negative story, to be sure. Yet, all the same, it makes an early impression on our consciousness that not only are we to not do anything to hurt other persons, but as children of God we are to care for, help and watch out for one another.

Even as we acknowledge that we know what God expects of us, we also recognize that we still are trying to learn the lesson which Cain (Bobby) learned so long ago.

Time and again throughout the Bible, the lesson of Cain is lifted up in both positive and negative ways to keep reminding us that as children of God and followers of our Lord Jesus we are called to love and care for one another.

Perhaps you have never made the connection, but the image of the watchman in our first lesson today is another occasion on which God reminded his people that they were responsible for one another.

In this case the responsibility is given to the prophet Ezekiel. Ezekiel lived in a time when the people were flaunting their disobedience against God and his ways. Early in the book of Ezekiel the prophet describes his role for Israel as being that of a watchman. He was to warn the people of their sins and that, if they did not repent, they would be overrun by the enemy and die or be carried into exile. If Ezekiel did as God asked him to do and the people did not respond, then God would not hold him responsible for their disobedience. However, if Ezekiel, as the watchman, failed to deliver the warning, then he would receive punishment for failing to be the watchman God had asked him to be.

Ezekiel was faithful as the watchman. He saw the evil in the people's lives and the approaching Babylonians. He warned them of what would happen if the people did not repent.

Of course, as we know, they did not. And our text today is his second reference to being a watchman. It occurs just before Jerusalem is destroyed and the people are killed or carried into exile. It seems that Ezekiel repeats his warning so as to remind the people that just because they are about to experience the judgment of God and be carried into exile, that in no way removes from them the responsibility to repent of their sins and return to living the way God wants them to live.

In this case God makes one person, the prophet, responsible for the moral actions of the many, the people of Jerusalem. At other times it falls to everyone as it began in the Cain and Abel story.

Imagine if each of you were tied by a rope to the person next to you. Imagine further, if I had you tie yourself together to the persons on both sides of you, so that we were all tied together in one long line.

In reality that's what it means to be a child of God and live in the community of people who trust Jesus as Lord and Savior. We are all responsible for the lives and actions of one another. When our sister or brother sins, we all are tarnished by that sin. When a sister or brother lives out her or his faith in a way that many see the love of God, all of us have reason to rejoice.

We do note that in our text where God appoints Ezekiel to be the wachman that God does add something that was not in the Cain and Abel story. We are finally not responsible for the actions of others if we have shown our care and responsibility faithfully.

The trouble is that most of us quit far too soon. We warn our children two or three times and then we "lower the boom." In the church, we feel some responsibility for others, but far too often we see others' troubles as their problems alone.

As I interpret what God says to Ezekiel and in other places throughout the Bible, our responsibility continues in some way or another throughout our lives. We are continually called upon to find ways to show that we care, to try to help our erring sisters and brothers see that God's way of forgiveness and love is a better way.

So imagine that a string binds you. In a very real way as you go forth in the name of Jesus and promise to live for him every day, it is always with you. Yes, you are your sister's/brother's keeper. Every time a sister or brother is hurt or hurts someone else, you hurt, your life is less than what God intended it.

How can you go on? Only in a daily walk of faith. When you stay close to Jesus, you can know that though your life is daily beset by the pangs and arrows of other persons who are not living God's way, your life is safe in him. Part of that life is living with and through the pain of being responsible lfor others. But another bit part is knowing that you can live and be strengthened in God's forgiveness, love, mercy, kindness, faithfulness, joy and peace. When you know the fruits of these gifts, then you will be able to care and love others for all of the days God gives you. Amen.

Proper 19
Pentecost 17
Ordinary Time 24
Hosea 4:1-3; 5:15—6:6

Find Your Way Home

It's 6:15 in the morning. Terry's alarm clock is screaming its high-pitched, pulsating sounds across the room. Terry, barely opening his eyes, checks his clock. That's it, 6:15. Terry would like to sleep another half hour, but he knows he has a busy day ahead of him. He tears himself out of bed and lunges across the room to turn off the alarm.

What day is it? It's Tuesday. And today? Today is the day Terry has been "unliving" his life for for the past two years. His stomach turns over and begins to churn. Terry heads back for bed but at the last moment he yanks himself up and makes a beeline for the shower. Today is the day his marriage will be dissolved.

Who is Terry? Where is Terry? Terry is one of the thousands of men, and women too because there is Annie, soon to be Terry's ex-wife, who every day fight the battle of knots in the stomach and keep a knife handy to scrape themselves off the floor now and again. A relationship cherished and celebrated has died.

Where is God when a marriage dies? Could it be he turned his back on these two on whom once he lavished such wonder, amazement, laughter, radiant faces, and, most of all, the ecstasy of true oneness? Terry and Annie had a large church wedding. For a while they worshiped together every Sunday. When the children came, they brought them to be baptized. And later to Sunday school. But then began the long, slow descent from what was once so beautiful and joyful.

Does God sometimes turn his back and leave us to our own misery?

Yes, he does. God does abandon his people sometimes. At least, there is precedent for it in our text from the prophecy of Hosea. God's decision to abandon his people on this occasion came out of his overwhelming perplexity with them. They had become so faithless, so wayward, that there was no way he could get their attention.

So it was that God had Hosea deliver the word that he was going to withdraw from his people until they suffered enough without him and came looking for him.

But how do you find your way back when you don't even know where you are lost?

That was Terry's dilemma. It had been over two-and-a-half years since he had been in church. God seemed so far away now that he wasn't even in the picture. God care about him? Huh, fat chance! If God really did care, he would have never let him suffer like he had.

Hosea echoes the words that God had said to his faithless people, "I will abandon my people until . . . they come looking for me. Perhaps in their suffering they will try to find me."

Where do you start when you're really lost?

Perhaps with a map.

Now, for a moment, think of what a map does. It helps you get from where you are to where you are going. But what if you don't know where you are? You need somone who knows the way to be your navigator.

There is a point at which, when you are lost and far from home — that place which feels safe and where love wraps its arms around you — that the pain gets so great you cry out, "O God, help me."

That's what happened to the people of Israel and Judah. They were hurting and they once again needed a place where they would feel safe and be loved for who they were. So they cried out for God.

It was Tuesday night. Terry sat alone in his apartment. There had been many bad nights, but this was worst of all. Now he was really alone. He began to have all the bad thoughts again . . . perhaps life really wasn't worth living anymore.

The doorbell rang. It was his sister Sherri. She reached out her arms and held Terry with a long and warm embrace.

"I know it's the pits," she said, "I've been where you are tonight. Now I've come to help you start the trip back like Sally did for me. Let's go out and eat. It's on me."

God answered his wayward peple. He heard their prayers of repentance. And like a loving parent, he said something like this, "Oh, what am I to do with you? You are trying so hard to please me, but your love disappears like the morning mist. It's here one moment and gone the next. Now listen to me. What I need is your steadfast love, not sweet sounding prayers. What I want most is your deep and faithful repentance, not your lovely liturgical 'burnt offerings.' "

The next Sunday Terry sat beside Sherri in the second pew. It felt so good to Terry to have a sister who cared enough to help make this morning bearable. "I hope you can find here the peace I've found," Sherri whispered, "God really does want you back. Welcome home!"

In another place in the Old Testament, God says through the prophet Jeremiah, "I will make a new covenant with my people . . . and I will write it on their hearts . . ."

That's the secret! It's not where we are that counts; it's whose we are that makes all the difference. We do have a map to help us find home. It's written inside us — on our hearts.

When you are hurt and displaced, remember whose you are . . . who to call for . . . and where you will find your map. Then you can find your way home, too. Amen.

Proper 20
Pentecost 18
Ordinary Time 25
Hosea 11:1-11

The Soft-touch God

Every parent who has children approaching or into the early teenage years knows that the day of reckoning is coming. The day of which I speak, of course, is the day when the once compliant, cooperative little girl or boy becomes the defiant young adult.

Many a parent among us waits with bated breath for the day to arrive. Not a few of us wonder how we are going to handle those times when our desire to care for and love our children openly clashes with our children's quest for a separate identity from us and their search for independence.

It is curious that the whole topic of childrearing and surviving the middle and late adolescent years of our children should intersect with our first lesson today.

The picture of our God which we see in this lesson is the picture of a God trying to be the loving parent to children who are just bound that they are going to go their own way. "When Israel was a child, I loved him . . . But the more I called him, the more he turned away from me . . . I took my people up in my arms, they did not acknowledge that I took care of them."

Doesn't it sound like God was trying to parent teenagers here?

In fact, the people of whom the prophet Hosea is speaking as he speaks the message of God are all adults, grown people, parents, people who themselves were the merchants, the shepherds, the priests, the leaders — all people who should have long ago lived through these testing years. But, no, now even they are acting like immature adolescents.

What's up? Who is grown up and who still has some growing up to do?

Amy is 16. Earlier this year she had the wonderful thrill of taking driver's education and passing her driver's test. At the same time her parents sat down with her and talked about the responsibilities of driving. They agreed that Amy, who had recently gotten a part-time job, would have use of one of the family's automobiles. She would pay for her own gas and insurance and help with the upkeep of the car she was driving.

A few weeks later Amy had her first "fender bender." It really wasn't her fault, so Mom and Dad did all they could to help her not feel so badly about it. They got the car fixed and said, "Let bygones be bygones."

Then after Amy had been driving three months, she let one of her boyfriends drive her car and he wasn't as good a driver as Amy. The boy's family paid to have Amy's car fixed, but Mom and Dad were pretty upset. They had specifically warned Amy not to let any of her friends drive her car at any time without their permission.

Five months later Amy had yet another accident. She was late for work and in her hurry, didn't look both ways at the intersection and pulled into the path of a car which had the right of way. Fortunately no one was injured, but there was major damage to both cars and Amy was cited by the police.

Amy's Dad became very upset when he learned what had happened. To vent some of his own frustrations and disappointments, he yelled at Amy when he met Amy at home after the accident. Amy was already feeling really bad about what had happened. But her father wanted to "teach her a lesson." Even as he lectured her, he had an inner, uncomfortable feeling that it was just not right.

God came face-to-face with a people who were set on doing it their own way. They were just sure that they could do it much better than any way God's laws would teach them to live. So they did — again, again and again.

There had to be limits on what God would let his wayward people do. Like a loving parent of teenagers, God had set limits. At times past he had punished his people because they did not follow what he had taught them. Now again he was being tested. "They insist on turning away from me. They cry out because of the yoke that is on them . . ."

What was God to do? It was clearly time to act. Was it time for a new revelation of his anger? Was it time to "teach his children a lesson they wouldn't forget?"

No, no, no! God couldn't do it. "My heart will not let me do it," he says, "my love for you is too strong."

So instead of blurting out his anger, God waited. He waited for the moment that his wayward people would turn and recognize him for the God who had created them, given them life and guided them every step of their lives insofar as they would let him do so.

It wasn't even a week after Amy's Dad had unleashed his anger upon Amy for her accident that he himself was in one, too. He too was at fault and was cited by the police.

When he came home that night, he could not even bear to look Amy straight in the eye. He didn't know what to say. Amy said it. She came over and put her arms around him and simply said, "I love you, Dad. It's tough to be a parent sometimes, isn't it?"

"Amy," he said, "I noticed in my last insurance billing that they are offering a refresher course on defensive driving. How about if we go take it together?"

They both smiled and shared another hug.

God very much wants to be a soft-touch God. Recall that softness of a bath towel when you step out of the shower on a brisk morning.

Oh, how much our own hearts yearn for the soft touch of God when we have been the wayward ones. And that, we must confess, happens more times than we would like it to be. Several times a week at least, if it isn't several times a day.

We can say at least two things about the soft-touch God we encounter here in Hosea.

One is that there really is a difference between God being our father and our own desire to be good parents to our children. We can certainly learn from God, but time and again our emotions will prevail and we as parents and children will say and do things which hurt one another. We need more of God's good example. We also need his ever-present forgiveness.

And we have it. As often as we seek it, he is already there waiting to forgive us and show us his mercy.

Second, the softness of God of which we speak really is not like any softness we know. God himself confirms that, "For I am God and not man. I, the Holy One, am with you. I will not come to you in anger."

There are no better words than these for those of us who are parents who desire to be loving parents and discipline out of our love. There are no better words for those of us who are children becoming adults who want so much to find our own identity and have our own independence and, yet, always have as one of the strongest ties of our lives, love for the ones who have given us life and brought us to the day when we can take our own wings and learn to soar.

We all need a soft-touch God and we have one. Amen.

A Note Concerning Lectionaries And Calendars

The following index will aid the user of this book in matching the correct Sunday with the appropriate text during Pentecost. All texts in this book are from the series for Lesson One, Common Lectionary. Lutheran and Roman Catholic designations indicate days comparable to Sundays on which Common Lectionary Propers are used.

(Fixed dates do not pertain to Lutheran Lectionary)

Fixed Date Lectionaries *Common and Roman Catholic*	**Lutheran Lectionary** *Lutheran*
The Day of Pentecost	The Day of Pentecost
The Holy Trinity	The Holy Trinity
May 29-June 4 — Proper 4, Ordinary Time 9	Pentecost 2
June 5-11 — Proper 5, Ordinary Time 10	Pentecost 3
June 12-18 — Proper 6, Ordinary Time 11	Pentecost 4
June 19-25 — Proper 7, Ordinary Time 12	Pentecost 5
June 26-July 2 — Proper 8, Ordinary Time 13	Pentecost 6
July 3-9 — Proper 9, Ordinary Time 14	Pentecost 7
July 10-16 — Proper 10, Ordinary Time 15	Pentecost 8
July 17-23 — Proper 11, Ordinary Time 16	Pentecost 9
July 24-30 — Proper 12, Ordinary Time 17	Pentecost 10
July 31-Aug. 6 — Proper 13, Ordinary Time 18	Pentecost 11
Aug. 7-13 — Proper 14, Ordinary Time 19	Pentecost 12
Aug. 14-20 — Proper 15, Ordinary Time 20	Pentecost 13
Aug. 21-27 — Proper 16, Ordinary Time 21	Pentecost 14
Aug. 28-Sept. 3 — Proper 17, Ordinary Time 22	Pentecost 15
Sept. 4-10 — Proper 18, Ordinary Time 23	Pentecost 16
Sept. 11-17 — Proper 19, Ordinary Time 24	Pentecost 17

Sept. 18-24 — Proper 20, Ordinary Time 25	Pentecost 18
Sept. 25-Oct. 1 — Proper 21, Ordinary Time 26	Pentecost 19
Oct. 2-8 — Proper 22, Ordinary Time 27	Pentecost 20
Oct. 9-15 — Proper 23, Ordinary Time 28	Pentecost 21
Oct. 16-22 — Proper 24, Ordinary Time 29	Pentecost 22
Oct. 23-29 — Proper 25, Ordinary Time 30	Pentecost 23
Oct. 30-Nov. 5 — Proper 26, Ordinary Time 31	Pentecost 24
Nov. 6-12 — Proper 27, Ordinary Time 32	Pentecost 25
Nov. 13-19 — Proper 28, Ordinary Time 33	Pentecost 26 Pentecost 27
Nov. 20-26 — Christ the King	Christ the King

Reformation Day (or last Sunday in October) is October 31 (Common, Lutheran)

All Saints' Day (or first Sunday in November) is November 1 (Common, Lutheran, Roman Catholic)

Bibliography

Carlston, Charles. *Proclamation 3: Aids for Interpreting the Lessons of the Church Year, Series B: Epiphany.* Philadelphia: Fortress Press, 1984.

Garrett, Susan R. and James H., *Proclamation 4: Aids for Interpreting the Lessons of the Church Year, Series A: Pentecost 2.* Minneapolis: Fortress Press, 1989.

Long, Thomas G., *Proclamation 4: Aids for Interpreting the Lessons of the Church Year, Series A: Pentecost 1.* Minneapolis: Fortress Press, 1989.

Norwood, M. Thomas, Jr. *Proclamation 4: Aids for Interpreting the Lessons of the Church Year, Series C: Pentecost 2.* Philadelphia: Fortress Press, 1989.

O'Day, Gail R. *Aids for Interpreting the Lessons of the Church Year, Series C: Pentecost.* Philadelphia: Fortress Press, 1989

Peck, George. *Proclamation 3: Aids for Interpreting the Lessons of the Church Year, Series A: Pentecost 3.* Philadelphia: Fortress Press, 1987.